THE FIRST NATIONS

GOSPEL AND CULTURES PAMPHLET 2

THE FIRST NATIONS

A Canadian Experience of the Gospel-Culture Encounter

Stan McKay and Janet Silman

WCC Publications, Geneva

Cover design: Edwin Hassink
Cover photo: Design on a beaded belt (Berkeley Studio, United Church of Canada)

ISNB 2-8254-1176-0

© 1995 WCC Publications, World Council of Churches, 150 route de Ferney, 1211 Geneva 2, Switzerland

No. 2 in the Gospel and Cultures series

Printed in Switzerland

Table of Contents

vii   Preface

viii   Introductory reflections

1   1. Aboriginal traditions, the fur trade and mission

12   2. The era of Indian residential schools

19   3. The transition years: personal accounts

29   4. Aboriginal self-government in the church

41   5. Gospel and culture from an Aboriginal perspective

Preface

The exploration of gospel and cultures is at the heart of our programme in leadership development. We work in a small theological school for aboriginal women and men in Beausejour, Manitoba, Canada. The influence of colonization and mission has created problems in aboriginal communities. Believing that an analysis and understanding of that history can lead to healing of fragmented communities and the empowering of aboriginal spiritual leaders, we welcome the gospel and cultures study project of the WCC.

Our approach in this booklet is to use the aboriginal style of telling the story. Not only is such a conversational account faithful to the oral tradition of our people, but it also invites comments or response from the readers or hearers of the stories.

Our experiences have been in a global context, with indigenous peoples all over the world. While this report focuses on a particular area in central Canada, it could be applied to many regions in the western hemisphere and would probably would find resonance among Aboriginals in the whole earth.

While our statements about the history of mission and the imposition of culture may sound negative to the reader, our experience is that hopeful change is taking place. New conversations are resulting in an openness for the future. We see significant opportunities to explore gospel and culture where we work. The process is at times painful but we think learning from history is positive.

Our faith in God and the love of the church of Jesus Christ enacted bring us to recognition of our shared journey with diversity. The Spirit invites us to the creative space of sharing life into the next millennium.

Stan McKay
Janet Silman

Introductory reflections

Stan McKay: Recently I heard someone read the parable of the fig tree (Luke 13:6-9), the one in which the owner wants to cut down a tree that has not borne any fruit for three years and the gardener pleads with him to let the tree live another year. I was struck by how differently people in the culture and geography out of which that story comes thought about gardening and trees.

I was reminded of what Adam Ogemow, an old Cree elder from God's Lake, once told me. Adam hunted, trapped and fished in northern Manitoba, and gave years of his life to the church. We were standing outside the church, and just over from the door was a large evergreen tree. In Cree Adam said to me, "That tree has saved my life many times." One autumn when he had been out in the bush, he told me, it began to rain and became very cold. Drenched with the freezing rain, he knew he needed to find shelter that evening or he would not survive. He went into a thick grove of evergreens, and in their shelter he was able to build a covering of boughs to get his body warmth back up. Another winter he had a similar experience; again the evergreen gave him one more year to live. Adam's experience, living in a difficult northern survival situation, completely turned the image of a tree around from the way it is used in Jesus' parable.

Janet Silman: Learning about traditional Aboriginal ways has transformed my theology. Already I am seeing things in a transformed way, even though that spiritual journey is still relatively new to me. I see much of Christianity, the biblical witness, in a clearer light. Our Christian theology can be transformed by traditional indigenous understandings. There can be a mutually enriching cross-fertilization between the two traditions.

From where does the gospel come? I think it comes from both traditions, although Christianity has assumed that gospel came only from the Judaeo-Christian tradition, with the indigenous tradition having nothing to offer. For me that is a limited and distorted understanding of God's power and revelation, and the historical impact it has had has been devastating.

SM: When I became conscious of my Cree identity and culture in my own journey of faith about twenty years ago, I began to see parallels with the tribal experience in the Hebrew Scriptures. That was only the beginning of a process, because what one still heard was, "You're a tribal people, but you're not Christian. That is the *old* covenant and we as Christians are living in the *new* covenant." I am still struggling to read the gospels in relation to the law and the prophets, to the tribal experience, because I too have been so conditioned into the ways of separating Christ and culture. It is taking a long, long time.

It is only in moments of real anger that I recognize that I have moved. It is hard for me to talk about mission within the old context, with all the garbage that the word "mission" carries for me. I recognize in that anger some movement in my own mind about what it is to be Christian.

JS: For all of us as Gentile Christians, whatever our ancestry — Africa, Aisa, Europe, the Americas — there are two "old covenants", two histories, two cultures through which God, the Holy One, has spoken. We have both our indigenous tradition and our "adopted" Judaeo-Christian traditions. For example, many people of British descent are rediscovering the Celtic heritage, which was suppressed, like other indigenous cultures, by colonial mission. What if we accept that the Creator has spoken from the beginning to all indigenous traditions around the world? Then they all have something in them of the gospel, the good news, revelation. When you think of it, if they did not, how would people recognize the good news in Christianity? It would be incomprehensible. It is clear to me that the cultures which are indigenous to this continent had some good news in them — some revelations of a Creator and of being a people of the Great Spirit — before the coming of the missionaries.

SM: The continuing captivity of "good news" to a cultural experience that is limiting and legalistic is an ongoing challenge for many of us in First Nations church communities. The fruit of the vine continues to be unhealthy because the vine is rooted in foreign soil that is not compatible with it. We need to do some grafting perhaps — I'm not sure what the image is.

There is a problem with the captivity of the imagination, the very spirit of who we are. So the years of the Hebrew people coming out of Egypt carry more and more mystery for me — the pain and challenge of that journey, the conflict that was in the community, why they could not get to the promised land quickly. I think about the struggles in the First Nations villages where our ministry students work. It looks like it will be a long journey of working to overcome our people's loss of confidence in our own stories. We continue to want to remain in captivity, to have someone else bring us the answers, because we have lost our culture, our identity as a people.

The question of culture comes in many forms. It has to do with state as well as church, with the vehicles of power in society.

1. *Aboriginal traditions, the fur trade and mission*

Janet Silman: In many Aboriginal villages in Canada where Christianity has taken root, different denominations are competing with one another, causing much conflict, confusion and pain. One way of understanding this tragedy is to look back to how the communities got this way. Many of the indigenous cultural ways, as the traditional elders say, have not been lost but forgotten. Yet that "forgetting" was imposed by an intentional policy on the part of the church and its missionaries to abolish Aboriginal culture and religion. What happened historically to bring the situation to this point?

Stan McKay: There were some cultural conflicts between our ancestors and those who came, but attitudes have fluctuated historically. At times government policy reflected the idea that we were going to disappear from the face of the earth. Then the newcomers saw our growing numbers and decided that maybe they had to help us adapt or change, integrate. Then later again the idea would arise that perhaps the Aboriginal people should go on their own and form their own limited governments. These shifts on the side of government have been confusing.

But the church has been single-minded throughout most of this history, which has been one of constant cultural genocide. This is not true of every missionary, but in terms of general policy the imperialist attitude prevailed. The church has been single-minded about what it meant to be Christian in North America.

JS: We could look at the fur trade. The Hudson's Bay Company had an ambivalent attitude towards the missionaries — not wanting them to disrupt trading practices, but seeing them as a good influence — but it was the Company that brought in missionaries with the first trickle of white settlement. Hence, from the very outset there was a connection between economy, state (with the Company also being the governors of the region) and church. Yet the

Company came here in 1670 and only brought in the first missionaries about 150 years later.

SM: The stories of the fur trade suggest that the patterns of the people's life were not greatly affected by it. They were attracted to the trading posts at certain times of the year, but that was not a radical change from the summer meeting places the tribal peoples always had, where the families would come and spend time together. The influence of the fur trade itself was somewhat limited. It was when the trade declined that the dependency on outside goods became a negative factor.

Many people make an issue over the Company's taking a great wealth of furs for almost nothing in return. That was a great injustice, but when the Company had a monopoly there was nothing for the people to compare their situation with. True, the ledger was not balanced in terms of what the furs were worth and the potential material benefit this might have meant for the community, but in another way this may have limited the impact on the community of the greed and individualism of the fur economy.

So I have mixed feelings about that early contact. As long as the people brought in the furs, the Company had no real need to impose a lot of outside values. In their semi-nomadic life-style, in which people had their own territory in which to make their living, the key was to be self-sufficient. The people did not yet need assistance of any kind. Each family looked after itself and the community shared whatever was needed.

JS: So there was not much need to change indigenous culture or religion, which remained fairly intact until the early 1800s. The same was true for the prairie region, where the plains tribes carried on much as they always had as long as the buffalo were plentiful. In the early 1800s the Hudson's Bay Company still governed the huge territory from the Great Lakes westward to the Pacific Ocean.

SM: For the Cree in what is now northern Manitoba, intentional evangelization began to happen around 1840. That was mainly because of pressures further south, with the movement of the Roman Catholic Church and the Church of England into the Red River settlements. Then the Methodist Church became involved. The churches made a "gentleman's agreement" to divide the region among the various denominations in order to carry out their mission.

The intention of the Hudson's Bay Company in inviting missionaries was to maintain loyal gatherers of furs. As white and mixed-blood communities began to grow and the fur trade began to decline, there were more and more people who needed some care.

JS: Before talking about "the Great Dying", the wave of epidemics which decimated the Aboriginal peoples from the beginning of European contact in the Americas, we should sketch a picture of life at the point when missionary contact began. Until then, traditional Cree values and beliefs had remained relatively intact.

SM: What the fur trade changed in the traditional pattern of life was the idea that "you only take what you need". This teaching of the culture was challenged by the fur trade. Traditionally, a family might take a dozen beaver from its trap line for food and for skins to use in clothing. Each season the extended family would very carefully manage all the animals within its territory. The fur trade changed that — when you learned that it took sixty beaver to buy a rifle.

I heard a story from Oxford House in northern Manitoba, where the old ways of trapping animals for the fur trade had been in existence for a long time. An old trapper came back from a successful season of trapping. In the trading post he brought some new steel traps. The following spring he came back from his trap-line with huge piles of furs, more than he had ever caught before. But he had come back convinced that this was not what he needed. So he took half of his steel traps, put them in a bag, paddled out into the lake, offered tobacco, the traditional thanksgiving, and dropped the traps into the lake. He kept only half of the new steel traps because he had determined that he needed only a certain number of furs in order to survive. This killing of so many animals was not what he wanted to do. This story illustrates some of the tensions between the greed and desire to accumulate wealth fostered by the fur trade and the traditional values of the people. It was clearly a struggle.

However, the idea did remain that for every animal, for each life that was taken, there was thanksgiving. If a larger animal was shot for food, there would be a ceremony of thanksgiving. There were also seasonal festivals. Certainly the feast of the late summer harvest — the berries, the wild rice — is still common.

JS: At Sandy Lake in northwestern Ontario, the blueberry harvest festival is celebrated even today by the whole community, including the churches across denominational lines.

SM: Another element is living each day in the season with the pattern of the sun: getting up with the sun and going to bed with the sun, especially during the summer months. Winter was the time of story-telling, of passing on the oral history. Among the Cree the winter was the only time the teachings were given — this powerful practice of sharing the traditions with the young, keeping the community educated about values and wisdom. In the north, with short hours of winter daylight, there were long evenings to sit together and hear the elders' stories.

In traditional life the roles of women and men would sometimes cross over each other, depending on the extended family. But even where the women were involved in such activities as hunting and trapping, the lines that marked out the roles of women and men were quite clear. In any case, the young ones would be learning by observation. The boys would follow their grandfather or father or uncle, the girls would work with their grandmother, mother or aunt.

The gift of children was highly valued where people were semi-nomadic, moving within their territories, and where life-expectancy was not high. There were ceremonies around the birth of a child. In the language of the Cree, a baby girl would already be called "woman" from birth, because she was a woman from the beginning. Talking to the babies was always seen as talking to the man or the woman. In some villages still today, the naming of a child is the passing on of the name of a deceased family member. It is a way of honouring the name, in a sense keeping the spirit alive, because the elders would see in the child something of someone who had lived before. These naming practices were also a sign of relatedness, connectedness within the community.

In the extended family the central value was that everything belonged to everyone. Personal property had a very limited place in the tribal community.

The morning prayers and evening prayers, the ceremonies at the beginning of the day and the end of the day were also a building of community.

JS: My experience in Aboriginal communities is that a strong ethic of sharing and of hospitality is still lived out. Another difference from European culture that always has struck me is seeing humans as a part of creation, not being over-and-above the other animals or separate from the rest of creation. This humbler understanding of ourselves as creatures is coupled with a profound respect for creation and a sensitivity to learning from everything around us.

SM: When describing the gathering of medicines, elders tell stories of watching what the animals ate when they were sick and what plants were safe to use. Knowledge about medicine thus came through observation, and once learned it was passed on through oral tradition. Certain people were chosen to look after those elements — medicine people. Also midwives were trained, keepers of the fire, ceremonial people — all these roles and functions were passed on to younger people who were given the teachings. The pattern of education in the community was well-developed.

JS: All those abilities were considered gifts, gifts of the spirit. Different people had different gifts and all were to live in thankfulness for those special powers, whether healing or prophecy, story-telling or leadership, humour...

SM: The women were keepers of the gifts of the community, balancing the economy so that food would be distributed throughout the whole community. There was always a sharing of food.

The idea that certain people have particular gifts also included those who had a physical disability of some kind. They were valued because they had other sensitivities, and these gifts made them all the more valuable to the community. As I was growing up, it was a very strong teaching in our village that people who are different physically, mentally or emotionally must be respected because they have something to give which the community needs to learn from them. That is a very old tradition.

JS: A current theme in contemporary theology is diversity, how we deal with unity and diversity. I think honouring diversity and learning from those who are different is a teaching much needed today.

SM: Another old tradition comes to mind. Many of the old people spoke two or three languages so that they could honour the guest. Even today old trappers or grandmothers still talk of the time when they would go to their isolated winter trap-lines and encounter another group of people. They would show their respect for one another by learning one another's language and caring for each other.

Depending on whose camp it was, they would welcome the stranger. That is a strong community motif, the tradition of welcoming strangers into your midst and honouring them.

JS: Among the plains tribes, even if they were traditional enemies with regard to territory, there was a strong respect for the other religious traditions. You could exchange ceremonies, giving a gift or a song or a teaching. The approach to other spiritual traditions among the tribes was one of mutual respect.

SM: Remembering this very old teaching of respect makes the present situation hopeful. People *can* learn from other peoples, can come to see that others have insights into good medicine, into healing ways. When trading for sacred things like tobacco, you would be in communication with distant people to obtain the tobacco which they grew.

Long ago when Aboriginal people in Manitoba went through a period of famine because of a decline in the food supply and a growing population, a group came from far to the east to teach them to plant corn. They also brought the sacred teaching about the ceremony of planting corn. Now because of the great climatic and great cultural differences planting corn never developed in our region. Yet the symbolism of the people of the corn coming to offer help to the people of the buffalo is encouraging.

JS: It is all connected — how we sustain ourselves physically and how we sustain ourselves spiritually. Yet in much of so-called Western civilization, stemming from the Graeco-Roman world, the physical and spiritual are disconnected. The spiritual and material, which were held together in Hebrew culture, were split apart in the way Christianity was brought to the Americas. The missionaries brought teachings about love, peace and justice; yet at the same time the "Indian wars" ravaged the plains and everywhere indigenous peoples were dislocated and their ancestral lands taken.

There was no connection between the spiritual message and the material reality, even though, ironically, "Christianity" and "civilization" were considered to be inseparable. By contrast, in the story you have told about the people bringing the corn and the ceremony of the corn, the spiritual and material were genuinely inseparable.

By the time the first missionaries arrived, the indigenous people had already had cultural contact for a couple of hundred years with Anglo-European fur-traders — English, Scottish, French. Besides, they already had experiences with many different tribes, languages, religious traditions. Against this background, how did they receive the first missionaries and the story of faith which they brought?

SM: To answer this, we have to take into account the influence in the Americas of "the Great Dying". During the 200 years of contact in the fur trade, our people experienced the coming of disease, with epidemics of various kinds — smallpox, measles, influenza. Along with the decline of the fur trade and the decimation of large game animals — in some places gradually, in others quickly — there was the coming of new settlements and the clearing of the forests. With all this devastation our people lost confidence in their own religious leaders. There are stories of whole villages disappearing, of everyone dying in an epidemic. There was a tremendous shaking of the spiritual confidence of the people. It was into this context that the missionary arrived, motivated to change these "savage" people.

So the missionaries came into communities where people were dying, where they had become captive in the sense of economic dependency on the fur trade, where many of their medicines and approaches to healing seemed to have no impact on their great suffering. When the missionaries came, they brought some relief from these new diseases; and the imagery of good news and salvation in the biblical stories encouraged the people to move from their old ceremonies to a new way.

Because of the language, the move to Christianity and European culture was never complete. There was some compromising of traditional practices in exchange for food. Asians talk about "rice Christians"; I am not sure what similar term might be used for the Crees and Anishinabe or Ojibway in this part of the world, but there were some acts of desperation in the search for a way to survive in the face of great suffering.

In retrospect it is evident that much of the gospel is about the values of the people. The tribal people already knew about Kitsay Manitou, the Great Spirit, the Great Mystery, God. The teaching of sharing life was a caring for each other and loving each other in community, which is what they had done since time immemorial. So it is not surprising that by the 1840s and 1850s the gospel was being carried up and down the river systems by First Nations people. It was our people who could speak the language, who had heard about Jesus, who carried the Word. The new medicines and possibilities for healing gave them hope. They developed their own understanding of what the church was and insights into what the missionaries were.

It is interesting that in this part of the country the churches with a more liturgical, ceremonial style of worship and dress were the most attractive. Many of our ways were denied a place in the new spirituality brought by the missionaries, but parts of the Roman Catholic and Anglican liturgies were meaningful. There were colours used in worship and smudging (incense). It is not surprising that the Roman Catholic Church became the largest mission church, and the Church of England was next. The Methodists faced a greater challenge. Despite their fervour for the gospel, they did not have the same impact, though their use of music with some rhythm did have an effect that lingers on. Because our own music was denied our people, the learning of gospel choruses and songs had an impact.

JS: To this day, Pentecostal churches are very attractive to large segments of the people in many communities. I used to be surprised by this impact of Pentecostal churches. Then it occurred to me how much the Pentecostal emphasis on the Holy Spirit and on the gifts of the Spirit, visions and prophecy makes sense in terms of traditional understandings: the Great Spirit, the life-giving power of spirit, good medicine and bad medicine, gifts that can be used for good or ill.

SM: I remember from my childhood visits to Pentecostal services in my own village that the music usually wound up with some kind of dance. The people would actually move to the music. When all our other dances had been removed from us — the Methodists especially did not permit you to move your feet when you were praising God — this took its place. The Pentecostals took some of the familiar gospel songs — some shared by the Methodists — and added movement and rhythm, both in body and spirit. Some Pentecostals would be upset to hear me say this, but the pow-wow dancing to the drum and some of the music Pentecostals use are not all that different in terms of rhythm and repetition. They would sing choruses over and over again.

Another element with the Pentecostals was the giving of a voice to everyone. The personal stories and testimonies in a Pentecostal service took the place of the traditional sharing circles and story-telling. Worship time gave everyone the opportunity to speak. That was liberating for people caught in the tradition of those missions where only one person spoke and everyone sang in a passive way.

So the various churches had different things to offer. Some churches developed models of shared leadership that are more successful in our communities.

JS: Recovering shared leadership is difficult when the "lone missionary" model is still entrenched in many communities. In our learning circles for ministry at the Centre we have found that while many Aboriginal ministry students value the shared leadership approach and depend upon the contributions of each person, others still fall back on the "lone minister" approach. I have noticed that this tendency is strongest among students from communities where mission has had the deepest impact. When students do learn to offer their leadership in a humble way, respecting the leadership gifts of others, theirs becomes a healing ministry both for individuals and communities.

2. *The era of Indian residential schools*

Stan McKay: By the end of the 1840s the churches were quite well established in western Canada. The historic mission denominations — Roman Catholic, Anglican, Methodist and Presbyterian — had all declared their areas. Then competition began between the mission churches. This heightened the tendency to cultural oppression, and devaluation of the culture of the indigenous peoples became a part of the aggressive mission efforts.

Around the beginning of the 20th century Indian residential schools — or industrial schools, as they were called on the prairies — began to be a central focus of mission. Young children were taken away from their families and placed in these boarding schools.

What the churches were finding was that as long as the people retained their language, something of the people's "pagan" imagery still remained. Before the establishment of residential schools, the missionaries could not succeed in driving people away from their traditions. I think that was especially true on the plains, where the people were strongly attached to their summer pow-wows and sun dances, and these and other ceremonies continued throughout the cultural oppression of the 19th century. Even when the government passed laws forbidding people to meet together, they continued secretly to hold their gatherings.

The missionaries recruited children for the residential schools in the period when my grandparents were very young. They would put the children onto the boat for the trip to school, and once they were on the boat, they might be away from home for ten years. They were conditioned in the church school to speak English, and they were trained to be the kind of Christian expected by their denomination.

Janet Silman: Not until recently did the terrible stories of physical, emotional and sexual abuse perpetrated in the residential schools begin to attract public attention. The churches and the government are only now being pressed to take responsibility for the devastating legacy of these schools.

SM: All the mission churches were involved. Their priority was in effect to carry out cultural genocide. Denying whole generations any knowledge of their culture or language by incarcerating children in residential schools was seen as the only way to make First Nations people European and Christian.

JS: It was heart-breaking for the generations of parents and elders who had to give up their children.

SM: Certainly it was painful, but in the eyes of the missionary sending the children away was the only faithful option. There was some coercion and pressure put on the families by the missionary. The pain was great for the families left behind, and even greater for those who were taken far from home to be educated, as it was called.

In the north the most intense period of tearing children away from their families seemed to be from 1910 to 1940. Then there was a sudden relaxation, and for whatever reason the government started building Indian day schools in the villages. I suppose this had to do with government as much as church policy (since the schools were jointly run by church and government).

Oxford House, in northern Manitoba, is a good symbol of the transition which came with the establishment of government programmes in the community. At first, Oxford House was only a summer camp. In the winter people would move in their clans to trap and hunt in their different territories. But in the 1940s the government began to enforce legislation requiring all the children to attend school in the community. A school was built in Oxford House and a teacher provided. The expectation was that all children would come to school, and as pressure was put on them, more and more of the families had to live in the village.

The men would go away and trap by themselves, so this became another factor in the erosion of the family. In the economy of family, it had been the younger women who were responsible for the keeping of the fire and the camp, caring for the children and always having food and tea ready, while the more able-bodied men and women were off hunting and trapping. That whole pattern was disrupted, because permanent homes in a year-round community were now required. In those years of transition it was very hard for both the men, who had to live by themselves, and for the families in the village, whose food supply had to be brought from the trap-lines a great distance away. That was a further erosion of the extended family and the connection to the land.

Often with the established day school programme, teachers were recruited who would also lead in worship and in the spiritual life of the community. It was not uncommon to have missionaries as teachers.

For a time it was felt that the day schools would do the job, but by the end of the 1940s the residential schools were being filled again — now more and more on the basis of the idea that survival in the world depended on getting an education. Many children were sent off to school because their parents were convinced that this was the way to be valued in the wider society. But the pain from that period was not different from that of the first wave of cultural genocide.

JS: All of this was being done "with the best of intentions", which makes me wonder what is being done in the name of the gospel today "with the best of intentions". No wonder many Aboriginal people who were students in the residential schools want to have nothing to do with the church or Christianity now. In fact, it amazes me more that some are still Christians.

Somehow they were able to recognize the gospel, the good news, in spite of the way it was delivered. I credit this more to the spirituality of the Aboriginal people themselves than to any particular genius on the part of the church. The church has received a lot of forgiveness from these former students.

SM: The residential schools were usually a place of incarceration, and they were run like prisons. The philosophy of education was based on a prison-like approach. Their purpose was to separate children from the influence of their family, culture and language.

JS: The children were not allowed to speak their own language; and the girls and boys, including brothers and sisters, were not allowed to speak to one another. The food was often not very good or plentiful, and children were sent out to work. Often the bodies of children who died at school were not sent home. Around some of the schools are all kinds of little unmarked graves.

SM: There are stories from the time when the schools were first opened of how epidemics of tuberculosis and other deadly diseases came into the schools. In many cases when children died their home community would not even be notified until weeks or even months later. The burial would already have taken place in some strange piece of land beside the school.

I think there was confusion within the churches and in Canada as a whole. The authorities could not decide what place the First Nations people should have in the larger society. When I talked to people in Australia, where Aboriginal children were also taken away, it was fairly clear that, at least for a period of Australian history, they were taken to be house servants. For the young men and young women to be good servants was for them to fulfil a worthwhile role in the society. It would seem that here in Manitoba — and in the Canadian situation generally — there was never a clear idea of what would happen at the end, after our young people had been educated. Where would they find work?

When the young people came back home after completing their education, the people in the village were often frustrated that the young women did not know how to sew or snare rabbits and the young men did not know how to fish or hunt. So they were no longer of any use in the community. They were a problem because they could not live from the land the way the rest of the people did. That may explain why for a while Indian residential schools did not have many students. The establishment by the government of Indian day schools may have been in part a response to the people saying, "These young people are coming back to us, and even though they know a few things from books, they don't have any value to us. They are a liability."

Certainly the churches were confused about what to do next. The residential school answer to "the Indian problem" clearly was not working.

JS: In the 1880s my Cree grandmother worked as a young woman in a Presbyterian residential school at Round Lake, Saskatchewan, near the reserve where her father lived. Although he always supported the sun dance, the mentality in the 19th century of those who were converted as Presbyterians was that you had to choose to live either in the indigenous world or the white world. Since the buffalo were gone, the pressure was to live in the white agricultural world. You wore Western dress; you opted to be Christian and "civilized".

The predominant ideology and theology seemed to be a complete fusion of Christianity with the Anglo-European way of life. A few may have questioned the identification of Christianity with "white civilization", gospel with culture, but the assumptions were so deep as to be "common sense". On the plains, with the buffalo disappearing so rapidly, the people either had to farm or die. In fact, some, like my great-grandfather, farmed too well. Because they were too competitive with the white farmers around them, much of their good land was taken from them and laws were passed that made it virtually impossible for them to farm. Unfortunately, the Christian church preached that the people should patiently accept the rejection and injustice they faced in the process.

Also, people who have studied the phenomenon of residential school abuse speak about the pervasive denial of the extent of the abuse, pain and alienation children suffered in residential schools. Some of my grandmother's nieces, now elderly women, will say, "Our residential school was not as bad as the other schools."

In any case, the schools very much functioned to distance generations of indigenous children from the traditional ways. The assumption was very deep that Christianity and the Anglo-European way were superior, that any intelligent person would choose that world and its values.

SM: There has been a long history of growing racism as our people became more and more visible in society and those who were educated began to compete for the same jobs. Your story from Saskatchewan reminds me of another one: some of the First Nations farmers did very well even though they had only small parcels of land. So the farmers around them decided that First Nations farmers should not sell their grain on the open market. That would make them competitors; they might become too successful; and that did not fit their image of the indigenous people.

As the communities next to the reserves grew, new racial tensions emerged as we learned the ways of the new culture around us. The most obvious racial conflict in this part of the world is between reservations and nearby non-Aboriginal towns.

JS: This underscores the importance of the issue of gospel and culture, because there are countless people carrying those racist attitudes in the churches of those white communities. The racism is so ingrained and prevalent it tends to be taken for granted. Historically in North America it is the

Deep South in the United States which has the reputation for virulent racism, but it is prevalent in Canada too. This forces us to ask how the gospel gets played out in racist Christians? Are racist Christians a counter-sign of the gospel?

SM: Some of us First Nations people are aware of gospel as something liberating, something that frees us to be who we really are. But the gospel's calling us into full humanity becomes very confusing in the light of tensions between First Nations people and the rest of society. The values and spirituality of First Nations communities continue to be in tension with the communities around them. The practice of holding lands in common and traditional ceremonies remain a threat to the outside communities and churches.

Even with the present cultural renewal in First Nations communities, this sense of threat and finally racism seem to persist in the dominant society. Despite the fact that the gospel was accepted by First Nations peoples, despite the fact that education was taken seriously, despite cases of success in the competitive European model of society, the acceptance is still not there at the end. That is the frustration which is very destructive. The churches have played a very significant part in that rejection. Many people in the churches know first-hand how difficult it is to speak of the gospel and see the racism and oppression in their own back yards.

3. The transition years: personal accounts

Janet Silman: We have talked about the fur trade and early mission history, and about the residential schools, which lasted until the 1960s. Perhaps we could bring the story up to the present by looking at your own story. What was life like for you growing up in a reserve community in the 1940s and 1950s?

Stan McKay: As I was growing up, a transition was taking place on my reservation — Fisher River, in Manitoba. In the 1940s a few families in my village were still refusing to obey the government laws that required children under 16 to be in school. While many families and clans would still go away to fish or trap in their camps on the lakes or in the woods, a few families would be left behind in the village. When I entered elementary school myself, many of the boys my age were away learning how to hunt and trap and fish. Although my father continued to hunt, fish and trap, his pattern was to go away and bring provisions back to us.

This period was very much a time in which traditional cultural ways were breaking down. It was then that the government began a rations programme, handing out small amounts of groceries through the local free trader, who would receive a certain amount of money each month in order to provide for families in which the father was ill. In a month they might receive six pounds of beans, a pound of tea, oatmeal, flour, rice, salt. This government dole was a sign of the erosion of a self-sufficient, self-determining community. In our family we never needed the dole, because my father was healthy and able to carry on working. But more and more families in the village were having problems.

Still, there were difficult times for us as well. As fishing became more commercialized, I remember my father having to work for the fish company because there was less and less freedom to sell his own catch. Gradually, the company began to have a monopoly. When there were lots of fish, prices went down, so my father would not make any money. When there were very few fish, prices would go up, but of course there were not as many to sell and he still wouldn't make any money. I can remember a couple of years when the fish prices were very poor and he came home from two months of work with nothing left over because he owed money to the fish company for his room and board. That was the kind of exploitation that went on.

About this, churches were silent. Since most of the people controlling the fishery resources were from outside the First Nations community, people had lost control of their own economy.

The church continued to function in the community, but it became obvious that the church and its worship life were less and less relevant to the culture. The church in my village, originally Methodist, had become a United Church after the union with the Presbyterians and Congregationalists in 1925. It still was a mission church, with a missionary provided.

When I was born, the missionary was still very much in control of the whole village. He cared for the "medicine bundle"; in other words, he had access to the medicines provided by government. He was a spiritual leader, but he did everything from pulling teeth to burying people to acting as a sort of magistrate or judge, the one who decided when to call in the police or other outside authorities. So the missionary became very powerful in some of the communities in that transitional time. With the elders largely confined to one community and less able to do their work in the clans and extended families, their role and power had been eroded. In this vacuum, the missionary became more powerful in decision-making and in people's lives.

A new element in many villages, including ours, was the breakdown of the former "gentlemen's agreement" according to which the early missionaries had decided that certain territories would belong to certain denominations. New groups were beginning to venture into other churches' territories. Conflicts began to erupt between Protestants and Roman Catholics, between evangelicals and the historic missionary churches. In the late 1930s Pentecostals came to Fisher River and established their own church at one end of our village. What had historically been a Methodist community was now divided in half almost geographically between the Methodists and Pentecostals. That division continues to this day. Other church groups have ventured in, but that has been the primary breakdown.

JS: What has been the relationship between those two groups over the years?

SM: Initially, the evangelical breakaway was an initiative from a group of elders who were challenging the domination of the resident missionary, who had become very powerful and was not leaving much space for the elders in the community to carry on their own spiritual leadership. The conflict grew to the point that some elders simply withdrew from the Methodist Church. This happened at the same time as the Pentecostal movement was venturing into the community. In a way, the breakaway was actually a liberation movement which led to the establishment of another church.

Relationships then remained tense for a long, long time. Until the 1970s there were significant conflicts over the different approaches to spiritual life. Only now are these differences being addressed in small ways. Only now are people beginning to talk more about the life of the community as a whole, and about the need for more co-operation.

JS: When you were growing up, did you go to church?

SM: Yes. The church was an active place. There was no access road into our village. We were an isolated community along the lake, with no modern conveniences, no entertainment apart from what we did ourselves. So the church was a gathering place.

Especially I remember times like Christmas Eve, when there was one Christmas tree in the village and that was in the church. The whole population of the village would come and pack the church that evening for the Christmas Tree Service. All the presents in the community were shared, usually one present per person which each family would bring for its family members. Nothing was wrapped. The gifts were things like moccasins, beaded mittens and jackets, mostly made by the crafts people in the community. Everything was handed out there in the church. That was the community Christmas.

Then at the new year there would be a one- or two-day feast, again for the whole community. The New Year's feast was a sign of self-sufficiency, of bounty in the community. Most people provided something, but certain hunters and women prepared particular foods. It was an "all you can eat" gathering, and for two days people could come and eat as often as they wanted. There would be games for the children; and the men would play a type of soccer in the snow. What a time of celebration! The Christmas and New Year's celebrations were the times when the boundaries between the two churches were crossed and unity was lived, when the old patterns of community life were honoured.

That too was eroded when the government decided after the second world war that the reserve was too poor to hold this lavish celebration. The Indian agent, through his authority, basically outlawed the feasting and the giving. The community Christmas tree tradition disappeared, though a few families began to have their own small trees, and the New Year celebration was ended. Only in the 1970s did the community regain some of the momentum of that feast.

The major factor is that spirituality, self-sufficiency and self-determination are always a part of our people's journey. You cannot disconnect the dignity of a people from their spiritual journey. That is the experience I had in my village as I was growing up. We were feeling less and less confidence about providing for our own needs, and there was an erosion of the resources all around us.

My father tells of the time when the fishing company came with huge gill nets on the lake in the winter time. He remembers the company stringing nets across the bay at the end of our reservation, basically closing off the run of fish across the whole bay — four or five kilometres of continuous net — killing the large population of fish in our territory. That eroded the fisheries from that time forward. Much as the buffalo disappeared on the plains, the fish began to disappear because of overfishing in our part of the country. That is an element of the historic exploitation.

When I went as an ordained minister to Norway House in Northern Manitoba in the 1970s, I discovered how important a role in maintaining the people's power was played by language. My own village had begun to lose the language because we were further south, and by then a road had been constructed and there were radios and telephones. Even when I came home from Indian residential school I could see that the language was disappearing in my village. To go to Norway House and hear the little children speaking our Cree language as they played was a tremendous sign of hope.

At that time the brunt of the cultural genocide had not yet struck. The people still retained their identity. Methodism was very strong, but a very strong eldership had also maintained itself in the community. And because the Cree language was strong, the missionary was never able to break the leadership style of the people. Whenever he made a statement, it had to be interpreted; and the elders could interpret it as they saw fit. I imagine there was a bit of subversion at times. The elders maintained control.

When I arrived at Norway House in 1971 and went to my first meeting of the church board, it was they who made all the decisions, as they had throughout the history of that church, even though I was able to understand and talk to them in Cree, the language of our people.

The elders were the ministers. I came into a situation where there was a powerful reminder of what the church had been, led by our own people. That certainly inspired me; but

I had to learn to work in my own culture with the elders of my own people, which was not something I had been taught in theological school. That was a joy and a gift, and I have experienced it in many of the northern villages, not only Norway House, where the elders were still strong. The women and men of the church took leadership, and in many ways were inducted into eldership for life. They served the church all their lives.

JS: What would the gospel be for them?

SM: The thing I learned most strongly from the elders in that early period of my ministry was something I had known as a child. They taught me again very clearly that life is gift, a gift of God. Their theology fundamentally was that life is gift and life is good. Every time a child was born in the village there was a lot of excitement. In this growing village of a couple of thousand people, the idea of the birth of a child was still a central part of their theological understanding of God's goodness. The continuity of life was the primary thing.

Related to that was the importance of community and the family, that faith is lived in context. It is not what you say, but what you do that expresses your faithfulness. They had not retreated into any kind of verbalization of what they believed; the faith was more what they did. It was their life-long commitment to service of one another, service of God.

There were still elements of feasting connected to the church. That for me was always a good sign. It certainly impressed upon me the nature of community.

And I was struck by their wonderful story-telling styles. The elders expressed their faith in the stories of the people. They loved the Bible, the biblical story. We had it in our own language, so they could hear it in Cree. Their faith was grounded in the biblical story. I was fortunate to know young trappers who went off on their own for a month or two at a time. The only book they would take was the Cree Bible in syllabics, and they would teach themselves to read it, especially the New Testament. They would read and learn it, then become tremendously grounded in the Scriptures.

This was a biblical people, more so than almost any other part of the church in terms of their familiarity with the biblical record, including some of the fairly exotic or strange imagery from the Judaeo-Christian heritage. Time and again I was amazed at how their imagination and spiritual depth enabled them to understand something from so different a part of the world and make it relevant to their own context. The women and men I met had a capacity for doing theology far beyond what anyone might have imagined. And so it made me angry that the institutional church was not acknowledging the tremendous spiritual depth of biblical Christian understanding these people had.

As I reflect now, probably the most hopeful thing was that, because the people kept the language, their cultural identity was never completely destroyed, even though cultural genocide had been practised everywhere around them from the beginning of contact. There were still elements of their culture being maintained very strongly because the people still told their own stories, like the stories of Weeseekejak, a trickster figure in traditional mythology. The legends and historic teachings of the people were also being maintained along with the biblical story.

JS: I remember in the late 1970s some people coming down from Norway House for a funeral at Swan Lake Reserve, where I was minister. Afterwards, I was told by some Swan Lake people that the Norway House visitors had been shocked that I as a United Church minister had taken some of the tobacco offered in the traditional ceremonies during the wake. At the time this surprised me, because the plains Ojibway community at Swan Lake took it for granted that I would participate in the ceremonies. It struck me then how different the communities of the north are from those of the south in terms of relationship to the church. Of course, within each region every community is different, but there seem to be some major differences between north and south.

The situation at Swan Lake is an illuminating contrast with both Fisher River and Norway House. The historic mission from the turn of the century was Presbyterian. Like the Methodists, the Presbyterians had residential schools in the region. Swan Lake also became a United Church in 1925. As I recall, there was a continuous missionary presence in the community until the early 1960s. But the church did not seem to "take root" there the way it did in many communities up north.

The story I heard was that the people were becoming increasingly dissatisfied with the paternalism of the resident ministers. Some ministers would not let the people into their homes. One apparently had a big guard dog to keep people out. Moreover, the United Church presbytery itself was becoming more and more uncomfortable with the paternalism of the ministry, so both parties — the church and the band council — agreed to end the mission in 1964.

For about a decade there was no United Church minister in the community at all. But this happened to be a time of transition when social problems were on the rise. Though surrounded by white farmers since the turn of the century, the community had maintained its language and much of its culture. This in itself was amazing, though part of the isolation that made this possible stemmed from the discrimination and racism around the reserve. With growing social breakdown, alcoholism and violence in the 1960s and early 1970s, the people asked the United Church to come back, but now on their terms. They said they wanted a minister to be with the community, but not to do Sunday services. It was to be a ministry of presence. The United Church agreed, and I was the third minister to serve at Swan Lake in that capacity.

I really loved the ministry there. Not doing Sunday services freed me to work and be with everyone, to respond to issues as they arose. I soon discovered that the band administration — at that time once again run by a white man — expected me to be part of the power structure on the reserve. The minister was still given a lot of power, and it was soon evident to me that most band members had very little power. But I had read a lot of liberation theology in seminary, and I used that social analysis to resist these vestiges of the old colonial power. I certainly made mistakes, but I think I did manage a ministry of empowerment, of encouraging people to find their own voice and claim their own power. We did some exciting things, and I soon realized people had a very clear analysis of what was going on. Before I left, the people got rid of the white band administrator — who had, in my view, abused his power — and took over their own affairs again.

But some people in the presbytery wanted to do away with the ministry because they felt it was not evangelizing the people. Basically, their attitude was, if the purpose is not conversion, why be present as a church? Yet I am convinced the ministry was about good news. It was certainly about healing — in part about seeking to heal the hurts which the church itself had inflicted on the people. It was about the church listening to the people. I had a good relationship with the traditional elders; we shared leadership in the wakes and funerals. The people were very clear that I was "their minister" and accepted me in an amazingly gracious way. I have never particularly understood grace as a theological term, but I experienced it in a powerful way from those people.

After a couple of years, they did ask for church services, which turned out to be Sunday School for the children. Yet even without Sunday School, in my belief, the ministry was valid. It was about reconciliation and good news. I think the church needs to be about repentance for its own historical sins.

An example is the people's pain and brokenness from residential schools, which is still being passed down generation to generation. Some of those who were abused in residential schools have become abusers of their own children. They beat their children just as they themselves were beaten in residential school. I have heard many people lament that they never learned how to be parents because they never experienced what it was to have parents. Churches need to face honestly how the sins of their own fathers are visited upon the present generation. To a degree that is happening in Canada, but the wounds are deep and the healing will take a long, long time.

4. *Aboriginal self-government in the church*

Janet Silman: The development of the All Native Circle Conference is a case study of how Aboriginal United Churches moved from having white ministers to having their own ministers and forming their own church courts.

Stan McKay: I remember in 1979 receiving a questionnaire from the national office of the United Church of Canada regarding Native ministry and Native churches. A number of us responded with some anger and frustration at being asked to take part in yet another survey and yet another study. But out of that came the first-ever Native consultation, held in White Bear, Saskatchewan, in the summer of 1980.

JS: I remember getting that letter too. I was at Swan Lake at the time. What I remember most clearly from White Bear is that two or three days into the consultation somebody suggested it would be good for the Aboriginal people to meet together for a time, and the non-Aboriginal people could meet at the same time if they wished. Some white people were very upset about the suggestion, while others thought it was a good idea.

As I remember, the basic point of the report back from the all-Aboriginal meeting was, "We want you to teach us the politics of the United Church, how it is structured and how it works, and we will teach you about our Native spirituality."

SM: That is about reconciliation. Behind that statement was: "We have something to give and you have something to share. There is a mutuality here." That was the beginning of a different mind-set from the old charity model of one-way giving.

JS: It was an acknowledgment that white culture needed something in the way of spirituality. I think it showed a recognition on the part of the Aboriginal people that the dominant white culture needed to learn something about the

Spirit, and that was something Aboriginal people could clearly offer. The dominant church knew the "politics", the knowledge and practice of power, and they had control of the church structures. The request from the Aboriginal side — to be taught about church politics — was very direct and to the point. It was a request for knowledge, not just for the purpose of understanding but for effecting change. And White Bear did turn out to be the beginning of momentous changes.

SM: About that same time I went to Saskatchewan for some meetings about the formation of the Dr Jessie Saulteaux Resource Centre.

JS: It is significant that from the very beginning of the Aboriginal self-government process in the United Church, the Aboriginal people identified education for church leadership as a key element. I remember Dr Jessie Saulteaux's story of being at a church gathering where she had thought she was going to be asked to speak. In the end, she was not asked. But she had a vision of little lights dancing over the people's heads, and she recognized the stars as young Aboriginal people rising up to be leaders in their own churches. Dr Jessie and other Aboriginal church elders "dreamed the dream" of indigenous leadership rising up in the church. There is something of the gospel, the good news, pressing to emerge here, pressing to be incarnated in the people's own cultural identity. The good news cannot be fully articulated by a people who are denied their own voice, their own leadership. The development of a learning centre run by Aboriginal people for Aboriginal people was a big step in giving the people's voice to the gospel.

SM: All those early consultations were focused on the development of Native leadership. In May 1982 at a meeting in Fisher River, my home community, where I was minister at the time, the proposal developed to hire a national staff person to co-ordinate this work. I was appointed to that position in October 1982. We had direct access to the governing body of the United Church. Gaining a voice in that way was important.

The national consultations initiated at White Bear had become an annual event. After a period of working through a lot of anger and healing a great deal of individual pain, it was becoming clear by about 1983 that this was a movement of people.

The circle image then became very strong. An executive planned the consultations every year, and the pattern developed of a cycle of meetings in every region and in the communities. Those were very powerful times of sharing. One reason for the strength of the momentum was the reconciliation that was happening as the various First Nations came together. Reconciliation between the Mohawk and Ojibway involved overcoming old political separations in order to focus together on the common struggle within the church.

The kairos moment for dealing with another historic mistrust came when Alberta Billy, a woman from Cape Mudge, British Columbia, was the First Nations' representative at General Council Executive. At that time everything to come before a meeting had to be submitted in writing about two months ahead of time. In order to be able to control everything that came before them, the executive wanted to have forewarning of it. We had always complied with that procedure — until Alberta Billy made her report at one meeting.

She had already talked to me and the National Native Council about the elders being silenced and the church being responsible in some ways for the silence of the elders. At the executive meeting, then, she first gave the written report that the National Native Council had worked on together. Then she put it down and said, "It is time you apologized to Native people." That totally blew the meeting away. No one was prepared for it. The idea was not new to the Native Council, but it was Alberta's decision to say then and there to the executive of General Council, the highest court of the United Church of Canada, "You need to apologize to us for the historic injustice."

Alberta had consulted with me just before she gave her report. We both knew that this departure from the prepared text was not according to the rules, but the executive also recognized that this was not something you simply discarded. The agenda had been altered, and the discussion started to happen in the room. A couple of people wanted to apologize right there at the meeting, but several others realized that she was not asking for an apology on the spot. It was suggested that we take the issue back to our National Native Council and plan a process there.

That ushered in the most exciting eighteen months of my five-year term on the national staff. We had a year-and-a-half before the next General Council meeting, which would be the best time for the church as a whole to take up the question of the apology. We were blessed with eighteen months to prepare, and we began.

We developed a pamphlet that was sent out to every congregation in the United Church to inform them of this upcoming request for an apology from the church and to invite them to reflect on it before General Council. Early in the summer of 1986, as the time of the General Council approached, I remember the elders sitting together at our annual consultation. People were buzzing, talking about what it would be like. There was some trepidation, some fear about what the church would do with our request, but by then the elders were convinced that we must ask the church for an apology. There was no question about that.

Some of us had a deep fear about what it would mean if the church refused to make an apology. But I have an image that will always stay with me. One of the elders said, "We will have the drum group come." There was a discussion about that; then someone said, "What if the church doesn't apologize?" The elders' response was, "Well, it doesn't matter. We have to dance whether they apologize or not." That positive framework of being a people, no matter what the church did, was for me the moment of a statement of liberation.

Our strategy was good. We met for about four days before General Council, at our own location in Sudbury, Ontario (the first time we had met away from a First Nations community). We decided that we would request the apology and then leave the hall. We would not take part in General Council's reflection on the issue, nor be cross-examined about what our purposes were. The apology was something for the rest of the church to discuss.

We requested the apology on the floor of General Council, then asked all commissioners who were First Nations people to come with us as we left the room. We went down to the sacred fire where we waited and prayed for two hours. We had a ceremony of tobacco offerings at the sacred fire. Jim Dumont, a traditional teacher, led us in a ceremonial prayer. The most powerful words in the prayers of the people that evening were: "There is nothing more that we can do than ask in a good way, and continue to pray for strength."

The evening of 15 August 1986 had been overcast with light, drizzling rain. But by the time we could see the commissioners walking down towards us, the moon was out. In the clear night there was a sense of things being well in the universe. The elders met with Moderator Robert Smith, the elected head of the United Church, in the tepee to hear what he would say. Addressing the Native congregations connected to the United Church, he read out these words:

> Long before my people journeyed to this land, your people were here, and you received from your elders an understanding of creation and of the mystery that surrounds us all that was deep and rich and to be treasured.
>
> We did not hear you when you shared your vision. In our zeal to tell you of the good news of Jesus Christ, we were blind to the value of your spirituality.

We confused Western ways and culture with the depth and breadth and length and height of the gospel of Christ.

We imposed our civilization as a condition for accepting the gospel. We tried to make you like us, and in so doing, we helped to destroy the vision that made you what you were. As a result, you and we are poorer and the image of the Creator in us is twisted, blurred, and we are not what we are meant by the Great Spirit to be.

We who represent the United Church of Canada ask you to forgive us and to walk together in the Spirit of Christ so that our people may be blessed and God's creation healed.

The elders' response — "We must go back and talk to the people" — had a great deal of wisdom about it. We danced with the drum. Everyone danced.

The public apology was an indication that the United Church knew it had made a mistake in condemning our cultural ways. Those First Nations church people who were reluctant to look at Native spirituality, or who were wondering about the church's position on Native traditions, now had some indication. Yet even now what the apology really meant is not completely clear. But it did give momentum, for example, to the development of the Dr Jessie Saulteaux Centre. The apology strengthened the Native Council, and that led to the dream of an All Native Circle Conference.

While the apology process was going on, we were discovering that although the church had not given us all the information about how it worked politically, we were learning from our own experience. Those of us who went to General Council Executive twice a year could see that we were in a state of "suspended animation". We were not finding what we needed in the existing presbyteries.

The conferences, the larger regional courts of the United Church, in which we sat were largely irrelevant to us. We had the National Native Council and its annual consultations, but they were making no impact on the political life of the church. Now and then we would make a recommendation to General Council Executive or other national church divisions, but we were having no impact on the future of our own communities. With that analysis, the National Native Council concluded that we had gone as far as we could in terms of informal processes. If we were to play an active part in the church, we would need to have our own structure, our own decision-making processes. In part, this also was driven by the need for our own leadership. As in all self-government, we needed to try some things ourselves. That analysis was the impetus towards seeking a conference of our own.

One presbytery, Keewatin (in northern Manitoba and northwestern Ontario), had already gone through a process of development as the first all-Aboriginal United Church presbytery. I attended the meeting at which they decided to become a presbytery. Rather than formalizing it right away, they decided to try it out for a year. At the end of the year, they decided, "This is complicated stuff. We cannot do this by ourselves." So they gave up. But a year later, after going back to their various surrounding presbyteries, they decided, "We can't take any more of this! The mistakes we were making were better than this!" They were finding their old presbyteries, when they went back to them, a total waste of time. They preferred to make their own mistakes!

Soon it became obvious to some of us that the models were wrong. It was not that we could not be a presbytery or a conference. We began to see that, as Keewatin had decided, we had no choice. If we were going to have any self-determination, any sense of involvement, we had better do it ourselves. But the model was still wrong. We were still trying to be a presbytery exactly like all the other presbyteries. That is where the struggle really began to take shape.

When the National Native Council saw what Keewatin Presbytery was doing, Keewatin became a model. The elders would come out for meetings, some not speaking any English. They would tell representatives from the other regions of the country, who had a good command of English and some political knowledge, how they were being the church. So Keewatin was a clear message both that this was what we had to do and that it did not matter what people assumed about our skills or capacity to organize our own church. Many elders from the north became symbols of that liberation.

About that time Christina Baker became the first woman from a Native village to be ordained in the United Church. To see Christina come into Keewatin Presbytery, which was mainly the preserve of emerging male leaders, and to claim respect, to take her rightful place in that body, was a powerful sign.

That was basically the story. After that we looked for a model that might be possible. I certainly did not have sufficient cultural insight to know what would work best, but the circle was well-established. The circle is a place where everyone has a voice and everyone is respected and included; where decisions emerge from a wide-open agenda, wide-ranging discussion and consensus — all things that empower people.

JS: And the large annual gathering each summer now became known as the Grand Council.

SM: Yes, the learnings from the annual consultations were recognized to be the way church was for us. That was really how we could be the church. We knew we could make important decisions by consensus. I still remember our identifying the four regions of the conference, making decisions based in part on identity and on the political realities of groups of churches.

We met for two or three days after the apology in 1986 for some debriefing. Already the politically astute among us were saying, "The next step is obvious. Now that the apology is made, we need to move to our own decision-making." In 1987 much of our council meeting focused on the selection of a name for the conference. In the name chosen — the All Native Circle Conference (ANCC) — the most powerful word is "circle". That was the symbol of the church: the circle and the cross.

By 1988, before it was formally approved by General Council, ANCC had been structured and the first two leading elders chosen. The formal proposal for the formation of the conference went to the 1988 General Council in Victoria, British Columbia, at which many other important issues were on the agenda, including a debate on the ordination of gay and lesbian persons. When the national church was preoccupied with other issues, the All Native Circle Conference was approved and came into existence.

JS: The inauguration of the ANCC did have a lot of meaning for those who were present. I remember many people returning from that General Council talking about getting up early in the morning and gathering at the sacred fire.

Occasionally, the ANCC has been labelled a form of apartheid in the church. Some non-Aboriginal people in the United Church are confused by this all-Aboriginal structure within the church. The striking difference from apartheid, of course, is that the ANCC developed entirely from Aboriginal people saying, "We need to govern ourselves."

SM: This again lifts up some of the traditional spiritual themes and values. When Keewatin Presbytery was formed, the decisions about how we were the church in terms of polity — making decisions by consensus, sitting in a circle, respecting each other, the core issues — were not made on a strictly theological basis. The motivation was not about cultural values or traditional ceremonies; it was about *traditional values*, about respecting everyone and giving everyone a voice.

In a sense, the ANCC *is* a form of apartheid in the church. In the 1990s the question continues to be whether there is a place within any of the historic mission denominations for the values First Nations people see as central to expressing their spirituality. Is there room for them to be people of God, to be Christian in terms of Aboriginal understanding?

We have also come an interesting circle on the question of self-government in First Nations churches. The question of self-government is now being raised in the Anglican Church of Canada as well; and some parishes in the Roman Catholic community have pulled away from the rest of the diocesan structures to establish their own church life with a form of self-governance. All of that may move further, I expect, but at the moment it is certainly keeping alive the question of what it is to be Aboriginal Christians.

In a sense, these moves towards self-government in the church are about separation, but in another way they are about survival. The values of the people are reflected in language and in respect for elders, respect for everyone in the circle. If you are going to maintain these values, you cannot operate with a polity that says: "You win by fifteen to fourteen — too bad for the fourteen people on the losing side, because the majority has carried the day." That polity does not fit in an Aboriginal Christian community because it does not support the life of the community.

We are living in an interesting time, and even as we talk about it I feel a sense of amazement that the move to church self-government has happened. For some of us, the issue now is also about spirituality, about the traditional ceremonies, about the openness of the membership of our denomination in general to our cultural realities. Yet it all started because we could no longer tolerate living under paternalism, in which others spoke for us and refused to hear our stories.

JS: What does the development of the All Native Circle Conference — and of parallel struggles for Aboriginal self-government in the Anglican and Presbyterian churches — say about gospel and culture and about the extent to which the gospel has been inculturated in the Anglo-European church systems brought to this continent?

SM: I believe it raises fundamental questions of how the structure of the church globally fits the pattern of oppression of the marginalized. It is important for indigenous people all over the world to look at their own tribal histories, which may mean going back a century or even many centuries. The colonial idea imposed throughout the world is that you structure the church around rules and dogma which judge people and so deny them a place as children of God. I think the structural question is alive for us here because of our attempts to change the historic oppression done in the name of the gospel.

I know that corporate structures have influenced the church greatly — the dominant social and economic powers that define success and control and "good order". All of those things are elements of a modern culture that denies so many people dignity and good news. It may be gospel that we in First Nations communities here have learned that we are no longer going to accept foreign structures and values. We are not going to submit to the obvious oppression in the name of gospel — not when our own understanding of the gospel tells us we must be liberated from this oppressive church system. We are going to give our church a shape which makes the gospel real to us in the context of our understanding of the Spirit of God. For me, that is a fundamental learning.

JS: The learning itself can be seen as gospel, as good news. If the container that carries the good news is broken, then you have to change the container. That is a very threatening revelation, because I think many people would like to see the gospel and culture question as something "out there", something that can simply be talked about, a kind of "pure theological reflection". In fact, it has to do with a critical self-evaluation and transformation of the very structures of the church. It has to do with who has the power and authority to define the gospel, to determine what is true and good, to decide where the lines are drawn and who is inside or outside the fold. The challenge is not just to people on the margins, but also to those at the centres of ecclesiastical power.

SM: This is one reason we are interested in talking with theologians in other parts of the world — in South Africa, for instance, where until the recent momentous changes the majority of society did not have any voice in government. What does that say about the church, not only in South Africa, but in all of Africa? It is a very large question.

JS: Part of *minjung* theology, the theology of the suffering people in Korea is, as I understand it, looking at the various indigenous religions in a new light. Previously, many theologians have acknowledged "the great world religions", such as Buddhism and Islam, yet looked down on the more tribal religions (which is ironic when you consider that Judaism, Christianity and Islam all have their roots in a tribal religion). I have heard Chung Hyun-Kyung speak of how shamanism was looked down upon as the lowest form of religion; yet that was often where women have found the most comfort and power. We seem to be on the verge of a global re-awakening to the value and wisdom in what were previously considered to be "lower forms" of religion. To me, there has been a tremendous spiritual arrogance at work in the theological enterprise in church and academy.

SM: It certainly gives us much to work with in our little Aboriginal theological school, because the process of liberation is such an important part of identity, of being a people under God. This was important for the Hebrew people, too, a people following the teachings given them by God.

This is a challenging and sometimes dangerous place to be. When we hear about the ethnic conflicts in Eastern Europe and elsewhere around identity, the need for spiritual teachings in the context of identity is evident. The two — tribal identity and spirituality — stand somehow in tension. The traditional elders' teachings about balance and respect parallel the gospel commandment to love one another.

5. *Gospel and culture from an Aboriginal perspective*

Janet Silman: We have talked about gospel and culture in its historical context in this region, and told the story of how Aboriginal people have de-colonized themselves with regard to the church. In fact, many Aboriginal people have little to do with the church today because of the damaging ways in which the gospel was introduced. Many who remain Christians also have a painful struggle in sorting out for themselves what it means to be both Aboriginal and Christian. It is a question of identity and personal integrity.

Stan McKay: The struggle of Christian and Aboriginal identity is going on in many communities. I am going home to Fisher River in a few weeks to take part in a "Wellness Conference" that some of the younger village women have organized. They want gently to approach again the question of what it means to be Cree and try to follow the Christian teachings. I think this is an interesting approach to a delicate issue in many indigenous communities. It is dangerous to venture into a straightforward discussion of being an Aboriginal person and having traditional ceremonies when you claim to be Christian, because it has not always been possible to bring the two together.

JS: One of our students who served as a minister on his home reserve this past year wanted to introduce some of the old cultural traditions. That led to some frustration. Afterwards he said he had been impatient; he had pushed. But, on the other hand, he opened some doors, so that now there are some people there who want to open those doors themselves.

SM: It will be younger people like that student who will be the ones to push and to raise the questions about culture and faith. I suspect it is likely to be the women who will have the patience to follow through. In many ways, it is a ceremony of healing we are looking for, a ceremony of the rebirth that the biblical image speaks of — a rebirth of values, of identity, of being children of God within our culture. The women planning the Wellness Conference in my village realize that this is a sore spot. They want to move slowly into the discussion and respect everyone in the community.

JS: When I listen to the elders who come into our classes or to our students from the North, I am struck by how the Bible is so intertwined with their lives. It is so foundational. When the Bible was first translated into Cree in the 19th century, it was really the Cree speakers who translated it, since they were the ones who knew the language. So the translation is a carrier of many traditional understandings. The missionary translators depended on the people themselves to find the right words, including those for key biblical terms such as sin, salvation, heaven, God. The word "Kitsay Manitou" was used for God. The people already knew Kitsay Manitou as their Creator.

SM: Our class discussions of gospel and culture have helped me to understand that when the Bible is translated and biblical stories told in the indigenous languages of the people, the culture itself has to be reflected, because the words come out of the culture. Because "Kitsay Manitou", the word we use for God, Great Mystery, Great Spirit, is of our language, the name carries some of the flavour of our culture. Some of the hymns carry similar images, although I wish more of our own worship songs had been kept. But the translated Methodist gospel hymns brought across something of the message as well, because of the form and imagery of the language. Concepts of angels and of the Spirit of God as present with us fit very much into a Cree understanding. Descriptions of the caring, loving God come through in the Cree language in a very helpful way, while we have to struggle with imposed concepts of a fearful relationship to a judgmental God. Although God is respected, some of the imagery, especially coming from the evangelical church tradition, does not carry the flavour of the language of the people.

We maintain something of the remnant of the culture, and the discussion around gospel and culture is a way of liberating some of that memory of our own stories. One day our spiritual expressions will be able to be explored without fear. Our language continues to carry the culture, and that is the key.

Another element to consider is the holistic approach to religion among the Cree and among First Nations peoples generally. It is not possible, if the culture is healthy, to separate religion from the rest of life; you don't compartmentalize. I'm sure you experience that in a place like Swan Lake.

JS: One thing I notice here in the circle is that people are only a heartbeat away from prayer. Often a prayer will be requested; someone is asked to lead in prayer without any advance warning. Prayer is much closer than I sense it to be in the wider society. People are always close to prayer because of their relationship with God. It is never a question of waiting until Sunday to pray or saying, "I'm not prepared."

SM: An element of spiritual life, evident especially where families and clans continue the tradition of selecting spiritual leaders from among the women and men, is the identification of those who are gifted in speaking with God. I remember a great-uncle who used to talk about a prayerful approach to life. He made long prayers in Cree — as a child it seemed to me that it would take him half a day to pray. He would pray for everyone over and over again. Yet that was an example of this prayerful way of life. Usually prayer is a time of thanksgiving for life.

JS: As with many First Nations communities, the church in your home village has a relatively small congregation. Quite a number of the members of the congregation are elderly, some are young people, but the church certainly does not have the numbers it once had. As in other communities, the traditional movement is strong. Some people might call themselves United Church, but not be involved in congregational life in an ongoing way. How would you describe the makeup of the Fisher River community now?

SM: What is happening in Fisher River is happening in many other places. The historic mission churches — Roman Catholic, Anglican, Presbyterian, United — have not been growing at all for some time. In most cases they are ageing faith communities. The percentage of involvement is down. The new emerging evangelical and Pentecostal churches have grown to quite a size in some areas. But the new presence is the traditional spiritual community of people looking at traditional ceremonies, seeking to understand our culture as a primary activity and not involved in church life in any regular way.

I think the writing is on the wall. If the existing churches are not relevant to the questions being raised by the younger people, if they are not inclusive of traditional ceremonies and story-telling, if they are not giving young people some vision of how to be spiritual people, how to fulfil their needs, then I expect that the church will cease to be a presence. There are signs of that already. I am not saying that it is inevitable, but I am saying it is a real challenge to the Christian community in all denominations to discover how gospel and culture are related. The people going back to the lodges and the traditional teachings and ceremonies are not finding what they need in the church.

JS: With our students here at the Centre, the ongoing issue that we clearly deal with in the circle is, how can I be Christian and Cree? Christian and Anishinabe? Christian and Assiniboine? How can I be a minister in the church given the destructiveness of mission history towards our culture? We grapple with that in different ways every time we meet. Our students incarnate that struggle. How are they going to minister? Can they work in the church with integrity?

And these are all people who have come here because they have felt a call to ministry.

SM: The wrestling has been going on among young people for about fifteen years, since the days when the Dr Jessie Saulteaux Centre was no more than a dream. People then were already beginning to ask, "How do the traditional teachings fit into my spiritual journey and my ministry?" They have wanted to know how the biblical story fits with our stories. When you open up the story of the tribal people of Israel there is a tremendous excitement in our community, which is a reflection of the people of God seeking to understand how we can be faithful.

We have experienced so much cultural genocide and so much spiritual imperialism. The church's history of indoctrination and devaluing our traditions is now coming unravelled. In addition to what we are doing at the Centre, the historical injustice is being revealed throughout the world today. People call the Centre a place of healing. It also is a safe place to explore our faith. To imagine a church faithful to culture and gospel is dangerous in the face of an advancing second wave of cultural imperialism and oppressive missionizing in our villages. That conflict is going to be with us for some time. Our centre can only be a launching place, because the real work is out there in the world.

Our community-based theological education follows an action-reflection model of education, in which students gather for studies five times a year and between those periods work as ministers in First Nations communities. That makes the Centre a place for finding oneself and doing the formative work, individually and as a community, that will allow sharing of the vision of hope and healing, the gathering of circles everywhere. The image of the circle is crucial in a society where we have been taught linear thinking and programmatic approaches that do not fit the spiritual journey of our people.

JS: It might be helpful to describe how the circle works in our classes. When I started teaching here about five years ago, a survey had discovered that people wanted more biblical studies. What I have sought to do in those studies is try to bring alive what was happening in biblical times and connect it with the present. So we do socio-economic analysis and history and talk about what is going on now in people's lives and communities. Everything that is important in people's lives is brought into the circle and explored for its connections with the biblical story.

While people are likely to have some sense of the damage done by the church historically, they may not have articulated this. But it becomes clearer and clearer in the circle, so that the anger and frustration surface. There is tremendous healing in that, but the process is a very painful one. For many people this raises the question, "How can I be a Christian, how can I be a minister in this church which has wreaked so much havoc on my people?" That anger is directed at themselves internally as well as outwards. We do that grappling in the circle. As the circle develops, there is individual growth and healing, but at the same time everyone is part of a journey together. I have seen that over the years. We deal with different issues as we go along, and the circle itself grows and evolves.

A few things have proved to be very critical in helping people to deal with their own issues of gospel and culture. One was looking at the apostle Paul and seeing how, in the early church of New Testament times, the big issue really was one of gospel and culture. Did converts have to become Hebrews in order to become Christians? That whole debate was one largely of gospel and culture. What Paul established was that people did *not* have to be Hebrew. Not that everything good about the Jewish tradition was to be discarded. Nor did people who were Jewish have to give up those practices, but Gentiles did not have to adopt all of those customs. If that had really been taken seriously, mission would have been different. It was here in the circle that this became more and more clear for all of us. Nineteenth- and twentieth-century mission would not have been the huge Anglo-European imposition onto life here. In that particular study of Paul I could see a freeing up of some of the legalistic ways students were interpreting the Bible, in which it became almost like an albatross around people's necks.

SM: In that process there is a definite liberation of the mind and the spirit to explore our own culture. The process is one of corporate exploration and challenge in the circle, and then monitoring our own individual feeling and growth. The experience is different for everyone in the circle. What impact do you think that has on identifying the nature of ministry as people go back to their work and do their own community analysis?

JS: I remember one person particularly from that class on Paul. She was struggling with other personal issues, too, but at that moment she experienced a powerful liberation of her own person. Some things had been holding her down, and there was a transformation in her when she went out from there. She spoke of it in terms of release and of finding her *self* for the first time in her life. She now works in an urban setting with people from the northern villages.

After her personal transformation I could see in her ministry the liberation of the Bible, its heavy law being released. She felt the joy and the awareness of the goodness she found in the Bible. I could see her going into situations with a new-found freedom and with an understanding inside her of the goodness of the traditional sweetgrass ceremony as well as the biblical teachings. She is sensitive to where people are in culture, and she has within herself a peace and a centredness that enable her to work effectively with people who are on different paths. And she can articulate all of this clearly, which also is important for her ministry.

I had a feeling that Christology is also a key for individuals working on their identity as Christians and indigenous people. If we believe, as I do, that there is gospel — good news from God — in traditional ways, what then is the newness that Christianity brings? I think in large part the answer is Jesus. How do we understand Jesus? The students spoke of "unlearning" distorted images of Jesus, images of an enthroned Jesus looking suspiciously like a European king, of Jesus silenced forever on the cross, of a pale, passive Jesus with blue eyes and blond hair. For many, that "unlearning" — or "deconstruction" in formal theological terms — was necessary in order to affirm images of Jesus with more meaning and creative power culturally: Jesus as healer, story-teller, teacher, guiding light, day-star, prophet — central images shared by the biblical witness and the students' own cultural traditions.

One of our students, who is also a student of the Anishinabe teachings of the Medewin Lodge, spoke of inviting Jesus into the centre of the lodge to enter into conversation with the traditional teachings. Here is a student combining his learning about the "historical Jesus" in contemporary biblical scholarship with his learning about his own wisdom traditions. That is exciting to me, and until now it has rarely happened.

During the week we studied Christology, some people went to a traditional ceremony. Coming back into the circle, one student said he thought he was in a Methodist revival meeting, because people were talking about what Jesus meant in their lives. In the context of evening worship, we were sharing in the circle what difference Jesus made in our lives. Was it enough? Is that relationship worth it, considering the difficulty Aboriginal ministers have in carrying the weight of the destructive things done in the name of Jesus? I can see students working that through, including students who at times say that it is not worth it. If I did not grapple with that question myself sometimes, I probably should not be here.

SM: I think that is the crux of the discussion in terms of faithfulness within the church after a history of oppression and judgment on our culture and our persons in the name of Jesus — history that in many ways is still ongoing. How do we continue to live as servants and followers of Jesus and the Christian way? That question is posed here at the Centre in the context of a supportive community. We sit in the circle and listen to each other attentively. Then we risk sharing how we understand our Christian calling. In this process there is a feeding of one another and an exciting nurturing of the shared journey.

It is always good, whatever course we are taking, to look forward to that opportunity of coming together to explore our Christian lives. We explore how we can respond to the people back home. We do social analysis, name those things that are oppressive, and that is liberating. The liberation process in Christ is a creative one. Christian discipleship does not give us a safe space. We live and minister out there in the real world, and we find ourselves in many difficult situations. There are so many areas of identification with the positive elements of our culture. It is a journey, and often a difficult one, especially for the women who have experienced such marginalization.

The social disintegration that we identify in our villages draws us into doing theological reflection on violence, especially the violence of men against women and children. On the basis of our Christian understanding, we are called to be involved. Or, to take another example, I am impressed by how people in our circle have been able to respond out of our culture to the AIDS epidemic. That is a healing ministry in a very challenging area that gives us much hope. With all the pain and ferment of transition, of re-examining mission and re-defining faithfulness in the context of our culture, we are moving into territory that has not been walked in before. We have begun a spiritual journey in this land.

The image of the Holy Land comes to me again and again. One of the great oppressions of us who are First Nations people of Canada is to hear one part of the world described as "the Holy Land". We challenge that here regularly because it does not take gospel and culture and sacred place seriously enough. The land on which you do theology is a sacred place. This is one of the great gaps in the theology brought to us from Europe. It continues to forget that we are bound to the earth and to the created order of God in the wholeness of creation.

To the circle we bring the stories of the natural world to which many of our people still have access. This connectedness has much potential for dreaming and visioning within the church community.

JS: Here at the Centre there is no question in terms of the gospel that cannot be asked. I think there is no question that Jesus or God cannot withstand. Often the church has told people, "You cannot question Jesus or the gospel or the teaching that God is like this or like that." Liberation is being able to ask our own questions. In fact, I believe we are called to do that. I am looking forward to our exploration of traditional understandings of spirit and Holy Spirit. I expect that this will be another avenue for discovering deep connections between the gospel and indigenous culture.

I often wonder why the Christianity which came to North America has been so frightened by the indigenous spirituality it found here. It has not wanted to see how the Spirit of God is already here. Part of the problem, I suspect, is that Anglo-European Christology has been too narrow, too limited to recognize revelations of God — the face of Jesus — in peoples and cultures that are different.

SM: The traditional teaching about respect for diversity does help in that area.

The possibility of diversity being a gift is frightening to a church that has been dogmatic and used words like "syncretism" to dismiss any involvement of people with the nature of the gospel. Any re-examination of the goodness of God in the context of many cultures and many different expressions of faithful living has historically been classified as dangerous or forbidden. Such questions are out of bounds. We are in a place where those questions *can* be opened up. For me, that is exciting. It means that many of the dogmatic statements have to be reread. Sometimes they may even have to be set aside because they do not emit a freedom or allow an exploration which is needed when the culture says that there is more in this area than we have yet heard or said.

JS: At a gospel and culture consultation I attended in Portugal there was a discussion about seeking a framework of language for discussion about the gospel. There seems to be a desire for some "irreducible core". That makes me nervous, because it is inevitably a matter of definition, and who is assuming the power to define? Language is culture. Language is logic. It is culturally bound and no human can get beyond that. Right there you have to decide whose culture will be chosen as definitive, as authoritative. It has been the Graeco-Roman culture. I think I would rather have taken the Hebrew culture — but the apostle Paul dealt with that early on.

Is there a common language? Maybe the common language is respect. Gospel has to do with our relationship with God and with one another. The question is how we can converse together. As Christians we need to be able to talk even with those people who say, "I cannot accept your Jesus." We as a church need to be able to reply, "Then we will seek to talk in your language. We need to hear and respect what you have to say even if it challenges and upsets us."

SM: Historically the church was particularly afraid of a form of mysticism carried especially by women. Those who recall the stories of the "witch hunts" in Europe and North America are familiar with that fear. What we are seeking at the Centre is to find a greater respect between women and men, a way of working together that in some ways has been lost. There has been a loss of balance. There is a quality of the spiritual mystery of God, the incarnation in Christ, the sense of God with us in person.

An important element for us in exploring gospel and culture at the Centre is to try to hold academic and experiential learning in delicate balance. We value both, and that is a new direction for theological formation. We have a model of integrated learning: doing and thinking, in which everybody has a place. Jesus' words that unless you come as a little child, you will not enter the kingdom, the place of sacredness, have taken on new meaning for me, because I begin to see in the circle that we are all childlike. Whatever we may have learned academically, whatever we may have experienced, somehow we find a common ground in the journey of the Spirit of God. We are led in various ways and given insight as gift.

Much of the mission of the global church has been about the powerful domination by the few who have the power of having knowledge of a certain kind. We are challenging that from an Aboriginal perspective and from a Christian perspective. Christ speaks to us about the childlikeness that we seek.

So the laughter in the circle is gift. The presence of little children when we are learning together has always been a gift to us. They too bring something to the nature of our learning.

Beyond that, the only thing I would add is that the tremendous fear of change is present among all of us. It is there among our people in the villages. I remember the anger some Aboriginal people expressed after the apology by the United Church of Canada. "We have learned this European way," they said. "Why do you want us to change back?" It was reminiscent of the Hebrew people wandering in the desert after fleeing Egypt. When things became difficult they asked Moses, "Why don't you take us back to Egypt?" Colonial systems which depend on institutional power and truth, including decisions by the institutional church, are well developed in many parts of the world. That is certainly the case among the Cree. The very idea that what *we* think and dream is good and right is a challenge, because it moves us beyond the prescribed truth.

JS: Gentleness and love and compassion are needed in working with those people who are afraid of change, even of liberating change. I see our students having respect for elders and others who fear changes and at the same time a passion to reclaim traditional practices and values and ways. I see our students holding those two things in tension. I am reminded of the student who confessed that he was not patient enough with his own people. Yet he learned from that experience, and the people learned with him.

Grappling with issues of gospel and culture is a lifetime journey for all of us. As our Dakota elder Gladys Cook teaches, we need to walk with one another on the path of listening, patience and respect.